TAMING THE SUN

FOUR MĀORI MYTHS

Gavin Bishop

RANDOM HOUSE
NEW ZEALAND

A RANDOM HOUSE BOOK
published by
Random House New Zealand
18 Poland Road, Glenfield, Auckland, New Zealand

www.randomhouse.co.nz

First published in 2004. This edition first published in 2008.
Reprinted 2011, 2013, 2014, 2015

ISBN 978 1 86979 034 9

A catalogue record for this book is available from the
National Library of New Zealand

Design: Grace Design
Printed in China

CONTENTS

MĀUI

AND THE SUN

"Let's go fishing," said Māui.
"Well, OK," said his brothers.
"But don't do anything stupid!
Last time you turned into a hawk,
and scared away all the fish!"

As the sun came up they set out.
But no sooner had they dropped
their lines into the sea,
than the sun set again.

6

"That sun!" shouted Māui.
"He is so lazy. All he wants to do is to stay in bed."
And Māui was right.
Each morning the sun would rise,
race across the sky
and jump back into bed again.

"I think I need to slow down the sun," said Māui.
"And you will help me."
So Māui told his brothers to cut a huge pile of flax.
Then he showed them how to turn the flax into rope.
And from the rope, they made a huge net.

That night, Māui and his brothers carried the net
to the eastern mountains where the sun lived.
There, they stretched the net over the mouth
of the deep pit where the sun slept.
Then they waited.

After a long time the sun rose from his bed
to begin his fast journey across the sky.
As he rose he got caught in the net.

The sun thrashed this way and that.
He saw Māui and his brothers holding the corners of the net.
"LET ME GO!" he shouted.
Māui hit the sun with his magic weapon
made from the jawbone of his grandmother.
"WHY ARE YOU HITTING ME? I HAVE DONE NOTHING TO YOU!"
shouted the sun.
"We will let you go, if you promise to slow down when
you are crossing the sky," said Māui.

"All right, I promise," moaned the sun.
Māui pulled back the net.
The sun crept slowly into the sky.
"Remember, Sun," called Māui, "I still have my net.
And I still have my weapon."

To this day the sun still goes slowly across the sky.
And there is plenty of time to go fishing
or to sit in the sunshine.

KAHU

AND THE TANIWHA

On each side of a mountain, between Rotorua
and Waikato, there was a track.
One track was short and the other long and winding.
A taniwha lived on the short track.
An enormous, man-eating taniwha
with bat-like wings and a huge head.

15

Kahu-ki-te-rangi was a young Waikato chief.
He was fed up with having to take the long path
around the mountain to visit his girlfriend, Koka, in Rotorua.

One day Kahu said to Koka's father,
"If I can persuade the taniwha to move,
will you let me marry your daughter?"
"Very well, yes," said Koka's father.
"Let me tell you something that might help.
That terrible taniwha likes to have his back scratched."

18

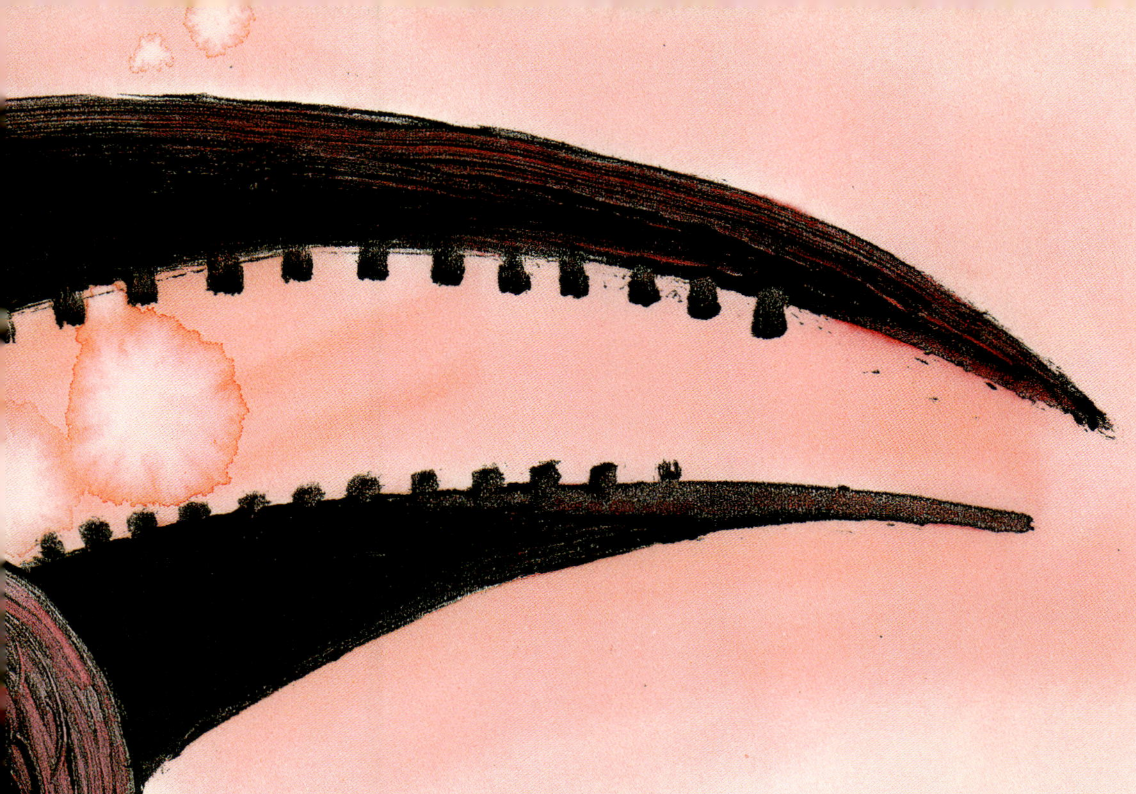

Kahu found the giant creature lying
in the hot afternoon sun outside his cave.
He quietly slipped up beside the taniwha,
and started to scratch his back.
"Oooooh, mmmmm, a bit lower," said the taniwha. "That's nice."
"I could find you a wife to scratch your back every day,"
said Kahu. "But you must promise to move to the
long path on the other side of the mountain."
"Yes, yes, anything," said the taniwha.

Kahu returned to his village and went to Pūkaka's house.
She was very lazy and dirty and had not combed
her hair for at least twenty years.
"I have found you a husband. He lives
on the short path to Rotorua," said Kahu.

"But only a taniwha lives there," she said.
"That's him," said Kahu.
Pūkaka thought for a while.
"Well, I suppose living with a taniwha
can't be worse than living in this dump."

20

21

Kahu led Pūkaka to the taniwha's cave.
"Now sneak in and scratch his back," said Kahu.

"Oooooh, mmmmm," said the taniwha.
He turned to see who was scratching his back.
"Yuk. You are dirty and messy!" he cried.
"But I will scratch your back whenever you want me to,"
said Pūkaka.
"Well, all right," said the taniwha.
And to keep his side of the bargain, he lifted Pūkaka
onto his back and flew to the other side
of the mountain to make a new home.

A few weeks later Kahu married Koka in Rotorua.
After days of feasting, Kahu and his whānau took Koka home.
The taniwha heard them passing by on the other side
of the mountain. He flew up and saw the beautiful Koka.
He was jealous and, in a great rage, he scooped her up
and flew back to his old cave.

Kahu was heartbroken and angry.
He gathered together a group of young men
and set out for the taniwha's cave.

The men made a trap for the taniwha
and hid in the bush.
Kahu called out,
"I have come to get Koka."
"Don't make me laugh!" roared the taniwha.

Kahu stuck out his tongue in a pūkana,
then sped off down the mountain.
The taniwha chased him through the bush
to where the young men lay waiting.
"Now!" shouted Kahu.
As the taniwha ran through the trap
the ropes were pulled tight.
They cut into the taniwha's neck.

As soon as the monster was dead,
Kahu raced up to the cave
and carried Koka out into the sunlight.

The people of Rotorua and Waikato were overjoyed.

MĀUI

Māui Pōtiki was small, but he was smart.
He invented some really useful things
and could do magic tricks.
But his four older brothers thought he was a nuisance.

One morning, Māui's brothers went fishing.
"Let's sneak away quietly," they said,
"before Māui wakes up. We don't want to take him."

AND THE BIG FISH

Little did they know that Māui was hiding in the waka.
When they had paddled far out on the ocean, Māui came out
from his hiding place. His brothers were really angry.
"You are a pest," they said.
"Sit there and don't say or do anything."

All day Māui's brothers fished. But they caught nothing.
Finally Māui said, "Let me try."
"Well, OK," said his oldest brother.
"One try and then we're off home."

Māui took his magic fish hook
made from his grandmother's jawbone,
and tied it to a fishing line.
He dropped the line over the side of the canoe.

Suddenly the line went tight. Māui pulled.
He had caught a fish and it was heavy.
As he pulled he said a karakia to make it lighter.
He pulled and pulled until the big fish rose up
out of the sea. It was the biggest fish Māui
and his brothers had ever seen.

Māui's brothers were very excited.
"We must cut up the fish so that we can share
it among our whānau," they cried.
"No, wait!" shouted Māui.
"You must give thanks to Tangaroa first."

But Māui's brothers did not listen.
They leapt from the waka and ran all over
the fish, cutting it with their axes.
The great fish twisted and its skin wrinkled.
Gashes opened and formed valleys.
Other parts swelled up to make mountains.
Many small pieces broke off and became islands.
The fish had become a new land.

"You fools!" shouted Māui.
"Look what you have done! Now, instead of being flat and smooth and easy to live on, this new land will always be rough and broken."

And if you look at a map of Aotearoa today
the North Island looks like a fish —
Te Ika a Māui — Māui's fish.
And the South Island is long like a canoe —
Te Waka a Māui — Māui's canoe.

RONA

Auē, that Rona was lazy!
Her husband spoiled her.
"Get me some water," she would cry.
"Cook me some kūmara."
"Yes, dear," he would say.
"Certainly, dear."

AND THE MOON

One morning Rona said to her husband,
"I feel like a big fish for supper."
"I'll get you one, dear," he said.
"I'll be as quick as I can."
"Take all day if you like," said Rona.
"I've got some sleep to catch up on."

Rona sat on the beach and watched
her husband paddle his canoe out to sea.
She rolled out a whāriki and
stretched out in the warm sun.
Soon she was fast asleep.
She slept all day, until the sun went down.

She woke up and lifted her gourd
to have a drink of water.
"Drat!" she cried. "This thing's empty!
Where's that husband of mine? I'm hungry,
and I need a drink of water," she whined
as she looked out across the dark waves.

"I'll have to get some water myself."
She picked up the gourd and walked to the creek.
Te Marama sailed overhead and lit her way.

But suddenly, Te Marama went behind a cloud.
Rona could not see where she was going.
She tripped, twisting her ankle
and bumping her knee.
Rona was very angry. She looked up
to the sky and cried out to the moon.
"You pokokōhua!" she screamed.
"You old cooked head!"

Te Marama stopped. He looked down.
He said, "Are you speaking to me?"
"Yes, I am! Look what you made me do!" screamed Rona.
"But how dare you call me such a disgusting name!"
said Te Marama.

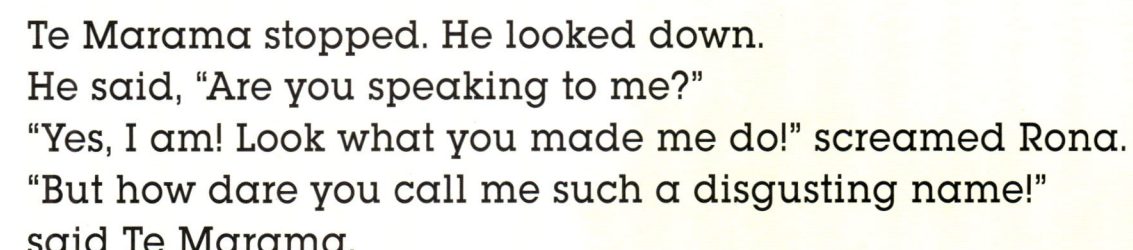

Then, without saying another word,
the moon zoomed down towards the earth
and caught hold of Rona.
She quickly grabbed the branch of a nearby
ngaio tree, but the moon was too strong.
The tree came out by the roots,
and Rona was pulled up into the sky.

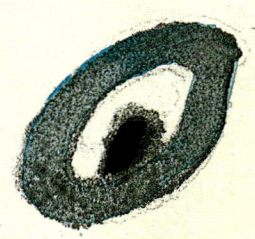

When Rona's husband returned with a fish
that almost filled his waka, he could not find his wife.
He looked in their whare. He looked in the bush.
He looked by the creek.
He went to the beach and looked up at Te Marama.

And there, on the face of the moon,
he saw his wife looking down at him.
"Come and see the big fish I've caught for you," he called.
But Rona only looked down sadly, and said nothing.

To this day, when there is a full moon
you will see Rona. She stands on the moon's
face with the gourd in her hand. She looks down,
still holding onto the ngaio tree.

When arguments start and insults begin to fly,
people still say, "Kia mahara ki te hē o Rona"
— remember Rona's mistake.